Report Card Comments

By Amanda Symonds

Copyright © Amanda Symonds 2022

Our Tips for Teachers When Writing a Report Card	5
General Phrases	7
Sample Template for Report Cards	13
General Phrases to Give Parents and Guardians	15
General Finishing Phrases for Report Cards	17
Demonstrating Progress with Examples	19
Academic Achievement	21
Attitude & Attention	23
Attitude to Learning	26
Art	28
Behavior	29
Citizenship	32
Group Work	34
Homework & Classwork	36
Independent Work	38
Language Arts	40
Math	43
Oral Communication	47
Reading	49
Science	51
Social & Emotional Development	53
Writing	55
Critical Thinking	58
Collaboration	60

Communication	62
Creativity	64
Goal setting	66
Memory	68
Motivation	70
Perseverance	72
Planning and Organizing	74
Playground Behavior	76
Poor Attendance	79
Problem Solving	80
Self Confidence	83
Shyness	84
Tardiness	85
Work Habits	86
The Above-Average Student	89
The Below-Average Student	91
The New Student	93
End of Year Evaluation	96
End of School Messages	98
Evaluation Not Possible	100
Useful Adverbs To Describe Student Progress	101
Useful Adjectives To Describe Student Progress	103
Conclusion	105

Our Tips for Teachers When Writing a Report Card

Report cards are an important way to communicate a student's progress to parents and guardians. If you dread writing report card comments then this book is for you.

We hope you can save yourself hours by using and adapting our phrases to suit what you want to express. These report card comments are a collection of all the things teachers might say about their students. They cover everything from English (writing, reading comprehension) to science and math skills like problem solving! I always try to give them a positive tone and convey what areas need growth or continued effort.

This book includes areas like general phrases, class behavior, homework & classwork, group work, end-of year evaluation, goal setting and motivation. It has been ranked and organized according to subject and positive or negative sentiment so you can easily find what you need to write about at any time! With this collection of ready-to go phrases you can enter them into your preferred software program or write the reports yourself. Please leave us a review online if this book has helped you!

General Phrases

Here are 40 general report card phrases to get you started:

1. Achieves most goals set forth at the beginning of the grading period.

2. Active participant in class discussions.

3. Always prepared for class with necessary materials.

4. Concentrates well and completes work on time.

5. Consistently produces quality work

6. Cooperative and works well with others.

7. Writes at or above grade level.

8. Displays a positive attitude towards learning.

9. Excels in problem-solving and critical thinking skills.

10. Exhibits leadership qualities amongst peers.

11. Follows directions well and completes work on time.

12. Gets along well with classmates and teachers alike.

13. Handles failure constructively by seeking help and trying again.

14. Has difficulty completing work on time/stays on task for short periods of time only.

15. Homework is often late or incomplete.

16. If given more time, could produce even higher quality work than what is already being produced.

17. Independent worker who takes initiative.

18. Is a risk-taker and isn't afraid to try new things.

19. Is always willing to help others in the class.

20. Is an active listener and pays attention in class.

21. Knows how to have fun and enjoy learning at the same time.

22. Listens and follows directions well.

23. Makes good use of class time and completes work on time.

24. Needs to be reminded to stay on task at times but is overall successful in completing work on time/stays on task for most of the day with few reminders needed.

25. Often daydreams or is off-task during class discussions or activities.

26. Participates in class and actively engages with the material.

27. Participates in class discussions and shares insightful comments.

28. Positive attitude towards learning.

29. Puts 100% effort into all schoolwork and homework assignments.

30. Quickly grasps new concepts and ideas.

31. Reads at or above grade level.

32. Responds well to feedback and uses it to improve future work.

33. Seeks help when needed and completes remedial work in a timely manner.

34. Shows enthusiasm for learning.

35. Sometimes has difficulty completing work on time/staying on task, but is typically successful in completing work on time/staying on task.

36. Takes pride in all schoolwork and homework assignments.

37. Understands and applies new material quickly.

38. Works at a fast pace and completes work before the end of class period.

39. Works well independently and with little supervision needed.

40. Works well under pressure and meets deadlines.

Sample Template for Report Cards

If you don't have a template to follow please use our basic examples below.

<Name> makes friends easily and is well-liked by other students. In reading, she has demonstrated skills in <specific area>, and with a little more work on <skill>, she will be reading at grade level in no time. In math, <name> is excelling in <specific area> but could use some extra help at home with <skill>. I can provide you with some recommended resources. If you have any questions or concerns, please do not hesitate to contact me.

<Name> is a hard worker and takes pride in his/her work. In reading, she has made progress in <specific area>, and with a little more work on <skill>, he will be reading at grade level in no time. In math, <name> is excelling in <specific

area> but could use some extra help at home with <skill>.

<Name> is a joy to have in class. She is always willing to help other students and goes above and beyond what is expected. In reading, she has made great progress in <specific area>, and with a little more work on <skill>, she will be reading at grade level in no time. In math, <name> has shown vast improvement in <specific area> and just needs a little more practice at home with <skill>. I can provide you with some recommended resources. If you have any questions or concerns, please do not hesitate to contact me.

General Phrases to Give Parents and Guardians

Please find attached your child's report card for this term.

Parents and guardians, the report card is a tool that can help you support your child's learning at home. You should:

Read the report card thoroughly and discuss it with your child.

Focus on the positive aspects of the report card, such as areas of improvement or praise.

Use the report card as a starting point for a discussion about how your child is progressing in school.

Help your child set goals for improvement in areas where they need it.

Encourage your child to keep up the good work in areas where they are doing well.

I am pleased to report that your child has made good progress this term.

Your child has worked hard this term and I am proud of their achievements.

Unfortunately, your child has not made the progress I would have liked to see this term.

Don't hesitate to reach out to us with any questions or concerns you may have about your child's report card.

I can provide you with some recommended resources. If you have any questions or concerns, please do not hesitate to contact me.

Thank you for taking the time to read this report.

General Finishing Phrases for Report Cards

Positive

Great job!

Keep up the good work!

You're doing a great job!

I'm proud of the progress you're making.

Good work!

You're working hard and it's paying off.

Congratulations on your success.

Improvement Needed

There's room for improvement in this area.

I'd like to see more progress in this area.

You need to put more effort into this.

This is an area of concern. We need to work on this.

I'd like to see you try harder in this area.

Let's focus on this area and see if we can improve.

I'd like to see you put more effort into your work.

This is an area where you need to focus on improvement.

Demonstrating Progress with Examples

Report card phrases can be a helpful way to communicate with parents and guardians about a child's progress in school. Using examples helps parents understand where their child needs more help.

Your child is able to confidently add and subtract numbers up to 10 and this is evident in their work when counting items around the classroom. You can support him further by asking him to create his own toy piles at home using counting.

Your child's writing has improved and they are using more descriptive language in their stories. A recent story included detail such as settings and emotions which helped create a vivid picture for the reader. You can support her writing at home by asking her to tell you a story about her day, weekend or any other topic she is passionate about.

Your child is making good progress in reading and is able to read most level one readers with ease. He is starting to sound out unknown words using his knowledge of letter sounds. You can support his reading development by reading aloud with him at home and talking about the stories afterwards.

In math, your child has shown an understanding of place value in two digit numbers and is beginning to extend this to three digit numbers. A recent activity that involved comparing the capacity of different containers was completed with confidence. At home, you could support your child further by filling different containers with various amounts of water and asking them to estimate the capacity before measuring.

To sum up report card phrases should be positive, brief, and specific. These report card phrases provide parents with meaningful information about their child's progress in school.

Academic Achievement

Positive

Your child is progressing well in school and is meeting most expectations.

Your child's academic achievement is good.

Your child is working hard and making progress.

Your child has shown improvement in their work habits.

Your child's attitude towards learning is positive

Needs improvement

Your child's academic achievement could be better.

Your child is not working to their potential.

Your child needs to improve their work habits.

Your child's attitude towards learning is negative.

Your child needs more support to achieve their potential.

Attitude & Attention

Positive

Your child is confident, positive and a great role model to others in the class.

Your child is an enthusiastic learner who is always keen to try new things.

Your child has made excellent progress in their learning this term.

Your child is able to apply their knowledge and skills across a range of different contexts.

Your child listens intently and tries hard to avoid the distractions around them, helping them learn effectively.

Needs improvement

Your child needs to work on their ability to stay on task and avoid distractions.

Your child would benefit from more practice in this area.

Your child needs to put more effort into their work in order to improve.

Your child would benefit from more focus and concentration in their learning.

Your child needs to work on developing a growth mindset and not give up when they find tasks challenging.

Your child is often disruptive in class and has difficulty paying attention. This makes it difficult for them to learn and achieve their potential. Please talk to me about ways you can help your child at home.

Attitude to Learning

Positive

Your child has a positive attitude to learning. They are always willing to try new things and they persevere when they find tasks challenging.

Your child is motivated and enthusiastic about learning. They are always keen to participate in class and they put 100% effort into their work.

Your child is a independent learner. They are able to work independently and they take responsibility for their own learning.

Your child is excited to tackle her tasks each day.

Your child always has a smile on their face when they come into the classroom.

Needs Improvement

Your child needs to work on their attitude to learning. They sometimes need encouragement to try new things and they may give up easily when they find tasks challenging.

Your child would benefit from more practice in being motivated and enthusiastic about learning. They sometimes need encouragement to participate in class and to put 100% effort into their work.

Your child needs to make more progress in becoming an independent learner. They would benefit from more practice in working independently and taking responsibility for their own learning.

Art

Positive

Your child is excelling in art and has a great imagination.

Your child is doing well in art and is very creative.

Your child is doing well in art and has a good understanding of the material.

Improvement Needed

Your child would benefit from paying more attention in art class.

Your child is very self-conscious of their work and doesn't want to show their drawings to classmates.

Behavior

Positive

Your child is well-behaved and a joy to have in class.

Your child cooperates well with others and is a good team player.

Your child shows respect to their classmates, teachers and the school rules.

Your child is able to manage their emotions effectively and deal with setbacks calmly.

Your child is always polite and respectful to others.

Your child is well behaved and follows all the school rules.

Your child is a good role model for other students in our class.

Needs improvement

Your child can be disruptive in class and this is impacting their learning.

Your child needs to work on their listening skills.

Your child needs to work on their ability to follow rules and instructions.

Your child would benefit from more cooperation with others.

Your child needs to show more respect to their classmates, teachers and the school rules.

Your child needs to work on managing their emotions effectively and dealing with setbacks calmly.

Citizenship

Positive

Your child is a kind and caring member of the class. They are always willing to help others and show respect to everyone in the school community.

Your child has made excellent progress in their ability to work cooperatively with others. They are able to take turns, share materials and follow rules when working in a group.

Your child is a responsible member of the class. They are always punctual and prepared for class, and they take care of their belongings.

Your child demonstrates good citizenship by following school rules and behaving appropriately in class and around the school.

Needs Improvement

Your child needs to work on their ability to cooperate with others. They sometimes have difficulty taking turns, sharing materials and following rules when working in a group.

Your child would benefit from more practice in following school rules and behaving appropriately in class and around the school.

Your child needs to put more effort into being punctual and prepared for class, and taking care of their belongings.

Group Work

Positive

Your child is able to work effectively in a group. They are able to take turns, share materials and follow rules when working in a group.

Your child is a good team player. They are able to cooperate with others, share ideas and work towards a common goal.

Needs Improvement

Your child needs to work on their ability to cooperate with others. They sometimes have difficulty taking turns, sharing materials and following rules when working in a group.

Your child would benefit from more practice in working effectively in a group.

Homework & Classwork

Positive

Your child is always punctual and prepared for class, and they take care of their belongings.

Your child completes their homework and classwork on time and to a high standard.

Your child is able to focus and concentrate on their work, and they persevere when they find tasks challenging.

Needs Improvement

Your child needs to work on their ability to focus and concentrate on their work. They sometimes have difficulty paying attention and staying on task.

Your child would benefit from more practice in completing their homework and classwork on time and to a high standard.

Your child needs to put more effort into being punctual and prepared for class, and taking care of their belongings.

Independent Work

Positive

Your child is a very independent worker and takes initiative in class.

Your child could benefit from working on projects with more guidance from the teacher.

Your child is very independent and is able to work well with little supervision.

Improvement Needed

Your child would benefit from working more independently on projects.

Your child would benefit from taking more initiative in class.

Your child would benefit from working on projects with less guidance from the teacher.

Language Arts

Positive

Your child is reading with confidence and is able to understand most level one readers.

Your child has made excellent progress with their writing and is now using descriptive language in their stories.

Your child has a good understanding of grammar and is beginning to use it correctly in their own writing.

Your child has made excellent progress in reading and can now read most level one readers with ease.

Your child's writing has improved and they are using more descriptive language in their stories.

Your child is able to understand and use a range of different grammar rules correctly.

Your child has made good progress in writing this term and is beginning to use more descriptive language in their stories. A recent story included detail such as settings and emotions which helped create a vivid picture for the reader.

Your child's spelling has improved noticeably this term.

Needs improvement

Your child is having difficulty reading level two readers. We recommend that you read aloud with them at home to help them develop their confidence.

Your child's spelling could be improved by practising at home with you. You could ask them to spell words from their reading book or any other words they are interested in.

Your child may benefit from some extra help with grammar. I can provide you with some recommended resources.

Your child could improve their literacy skills by reading more at home.
Your child is having difficulty reading level two readers. We recommend practising at home with your child.

Your child could improve their writing by including more details in their stories. You could ask them to tell you a story about their day, weekend or any other topic they are passionate about.

Your child may benefit from some extra help with grammar. I can provide you with some recommended resources.

Math

Positive

Uses different strategies to solve one or two step problems.

Your child has a strong understanding of place value and is able to apply this knowledge in different contexts.

Demonstrates a good understanding of math concepts.

Your child can fluently add and subtract two-digit numbers and is beginning to extend this to three-digit numbers.

Your child has made excellent progress with their times tables and can now recall them with ease.

Your child uses a range of strategies when solving problems, including both mental and written methods.

Your child is confident and competent in math. They are able to solve a variety of problems accurately and efficiently.

Your child has made excellent progress in their math class this term.

Your child is able to apply their knowledge and skills across a range of different contexts.

Needs Improvement

Your child needs to work on their confidence and competence in math. They sometimes struggle with solving problems accurately and efficiently.

Your child is having difficulty solving math questions that involve word problems.

Has difficulty understanding math word problems.

Your child is struggling to remember their times tables. We recommend buying a poster and practising them at home with your child.

Your child is having difficulty understanding place value. We recommend using everyday objects to help them understand the concept.

Needs to slow down and check their work.

Your child could improve their problem-solving skills by practising at home with you.

Your child needs to work on their number fluency and being able to recall math facts quickly.

Your child would benefit from more math practise at home.

Your child needs to work on applying their knowledge and skills across a range of different contexts.

Has difficulty solving multi step problems.

Memorizing basic math facts would be helpful.

Oral Communication

Positive

Your child is confident and articulate when communicating with others. They are able to express their ideas clearly and they listen attentively to others.

Your child has made excellent progress in their oral communication this term.

Your child is able to use a range of vocabulary and sentence structures when speaking.

Needs Improvement

Your child needs to work on their confidence and articulation when communicating with others. They sometimes have difficulty expressing their ideas clearly and they may not always listen attentively to others.

Your child would benefit from more progress in their oral communication this term.

Your child needs to work on using a range of vocabulary and sentence structures when speaking.

Reading

Positive

Your child is a competent and confident reader. They are able to read a variety of texts accurately and fluently.

Has good reading and decoding skills.

Your child has made excellent progress in their reading this term.

Is reading smoothly with good expression.

Your child is able to understand and critically evaluate what they have read.

Is choosing books that are too simple for his / her level.

Needs Improvement

Struggles with reading comprehension.

Your child needs to work on their ability to read accurately and fluently. They sometimes struggle with reading unfamiliar words and they may not read at a consistent pace.

Your child would benefit from more progress in their reading this term.

I would like to see (name) read for 15 minutes each night.

Needs to learn sight words to improve decoding skills.

Your child needs to work on understanding and critically evaluating what they have read. They may need help to identify the main ideas in a text or to make inferences about what they have read.

Science

Positive

Your child is excelling in science and answers questions thoughtfully in class.

Your child is doing well in science and has a good understanding of the material.

Your child is doing well in science and is a pleasure to teach in the classroom.

Improvement Needed

Your child could benefit from reviewing the material more thoroughly.

Your child would benefit from paying more attention in science class.

Your child would benefit from participating more in class.

Social & Emotional Development

Positive

Your child is able to manage their emotions effectively and cope well in challenging situations.

Your child is a kind and caring person who is always willing to help others.

Your child has made excellent progress in developing their social skills and is now able to interact confidently with others.

Your child is confident and has a good self-esteem.

Your child is able to manage their emotions effectively.

Your child has made good progress in their social and emotional development.

Needs improvement

Your child sometimes struggles to control their emotions, particularly when they are feeling frustrated. We recommend providing them with some tools to help them cope, such as deep breathing or counting to 10.

Your child may benefit from some extra help with social skills. I can provide you with some recommended resources.

Your child needs to work on their self-esteem.

Your child would benefit from more practice in managing their emotions effectively.

Your child needs support from you to make more progress in their social and emotional development.

Writing

Positive

Your child is a competent and confident writer. They are able to write a variety of texts accurately and fluently.

Your child has made excellent progress in their writing this term.

Your child is able to use a range of vocabulary and sentence structures in their writing.

Is willing to lear new writing skills and quickly apply these skills in his / her writing.

Writing is clear and following grammar and punctuation skills.

Enjoys writing and can construct interesting sentences for the reader.

Needs Improvement

Your child needs to work on their ability to write accurately and fluently. They sometimes struggle with putting their ideas into writing or they may not write at a consistent pace.

Your child would benefit from more progress in their writing this term.

Your child needs to work on using a range of vocabulary and sentence structures in their writing.

Words are often misplaced throughout his / her writing.

Needs to spend additional time proofreading his / her work for errors before handing it in.

Needs to spend additional time ensuring their work is legible and easy to read.

Frequently displays grammatically errors within. his / her writing.

Needs to spend additional time planning or organizing their ideas before writing.

Needs to spend additional time paying attention to detail when writing.

Critical Thinking

Positive

Your child is able to think critically and creatively. They are able to identify problems and find solutions.

Your child has made excellent progress in their critical thinking this term.

Your child is able to apply their critical thinking skills across a range of different contexts.

Needs Improvement

Your child needs to work on their ability to think critically and creatively. They sometimes struggle with identifying problems or finding solutions.

Your child would benefit from more progress in their critical thinking this term.

Your child needs to work on applying their critical thinking skills across a range of different contexts.

Collaboration

Positive

Your child is able to work effectively in a team. They are able to share ideas and resources, and they work well with others.

Your child has made excellent progress in their collaboration this term.

Your child is able to apply their collaborative skills across a range of different contexts.

Needs Improvement

Your child needs to work on their ability to work effectively in a team. They sometimes struggle with sharing ideas and resources, or they may not work well with others.

Your child would benefit from more progress in their collaboration this term.

Your child needs to work on applying their collaborative skills across a range of different contexts.

Communication

Positive

Your child is an effective communicator. They are able to express their ideas clearly and confidently.

Your child has made excellent progress in their communication this term.

Your child is able to apply their communication skills across a range of different contexts.

Needs Improvement

Needs to work on their ability to communicate effectively. They sometimes struggle with expressing their ideas clearly and confidently.

Needs to actively participate in classroom discussion.

Your child would benefit from more progress in their communication this term.

Your child needs to work on applying their communication skills across a range of different contexts.

Eager to participate but needs to raise his / her hand in class.

One area for improvement is

Creativity

Positive

Your child is creative and imaginative. They are able to come up with new ideas and think outside the box.

Your child has made excellent progress in their creativity this term.

Your child is able to apply their creative skills across a range of different contexts.

Needs Improvement

Your child needs to work on their creativity and imagination. They sometimes struggle with coming up with new and original ideas.

Your child would benefit from more progress in their creativity this term.

Your child needs to work on applying their creative skills across a range of different contexts.

Your child needs to work on their creativity. They sometimes struggle with coming up with new ideas or thinking outside the box.

Goal setting

Positive

Your child has set realistic goals for themselves and is working hard to achieve them.

Your child has set high goals for themselves and is working hard to achieve them.

Your child would benefit from setting more specific goals for themselves.

Improvement Needed

Your child would benefit from setting more realistic goals for themselves.

Your child would benefit from setting higher goals for themselves.

Your child would benefit from setting more specific goals for themselves.

Memory

Positive

Your child has a great memory. They are able to remember information and recall it when they need to.

Your child has made excellent progress in their memory this term.

Your child is able to apply their memory skills across a range of different contexts.

Needs Improvement

Your child needs to work on their memory. They sometimes struggle with remembering information or recalling it when they need to.

Your child would benefit from more progress in their memory this term.

Your child needs to work on applying their memory skills across a range of different contexts.

Motivation

Positive

Your child is highly motivated in their learning and is always keen to try new things.

Your child has made excellent progress in their learning this term.

Your child is able to apply their knowledge and skills across a range of different contexts.

Needs Improvement

Your child needs to work on their motivation in their learning.

Your child would benefit from more motivation to make progress in their learning this term.

Your child needs to work on their ability to apply their knowledge and skills across a range of different contexts.

Perseverance

Positive

Your child is able to persevere through challenges. They are able to keep trying even when they find something difficult.

Your child has made excellent progress in their perseverance this term.

Your child is able to apply their perseverance skills across a range of different contexts.

Needs Improvement

Your child needs to work on their ability to persevere through challenges. They sometimes struggle with keeping trying even when they find something difficult.

Your child would benefit from more progress in their perseverance this term.

Your child needs to work on applying their perseverance skills across a range of different contexts.

Planning and Organizing

Positive

Your child is able to plan and organise their work effectively. They are able to set goals and meet deadlines.

Your child has made excellent progress in their planning and organisation this term.

Your child is able to apply their planning and organizing skills across a range of different contexts.

Needs Improvement

Your child needs to work on their ability to plan and organise their work effectively. They sometimes struggle with setting goals or meeting deadlines.

Your child would benefit from more progress in their planning and organisation this term.

Your child needs to work on applying their planning and organizing skills across a range of different contexts.

Playground Behavior

Positive

Your child is a good role model to others on the playground. They follow the rules and help to keep everyone safe.

Your child is able to work well with others on the playground. They share materials, take turns and cooperate when playing games.

Your child demonstrates appropriate social skills on the playground. They interact politely with other children and adults.

Your child is a pleasant person to be around on the playground. They are friendly and cheerful, and they make others feel welcome.

Needs Improvement

Your child needs to work on their ability to follow the rules on the playground. They sometimes forget and need reminders about what is expected.

Your child would benefit from more practice in following the rules on the playground.

Your child needs to put more effort into being a good role model to others on the playground. They should try to set a good example for others to follow.

Your child could improve their social skills on the playground by interacting more politely with other children and adults.

Your child could be more cheerful and friendly on the playground. They should try to make others feel welcome.

Poor Attendance

Needs improvement

Your child has been absent for a significant number of days and this has impacted their learning.

Your child's health has improved since the last report, but they are still missing school regularly. This is impacting their learning.

Your child's attendance has not improved and they are still missing a lot of school. This is having a negative impact on their learning.

Your child has been absent for a significant number of days and this has impacted their learning. Your child needs to improve their attendance if they want to make progress in school.

Problem Solving

Positive

Your child is able to solve problems effectively. They are able to identify issues and find solutions.

Your child has made excellent progress in their problem solving this term.

Your child is able to apply their problem solving skills across a range of different contexts.

Your child is able to solve problems independently and is often able to find more than one solution to a problem.

Your child is beginning to think creatively when solving problems and is not afraid to try new things.

Your child works well with others and is able to share ideas and reach a consensus.

Needs Improvement

Your child needs to work on their ability to solve problems effectively. They sometimes struggle with identifying issues or finding solutions.

Your child would benefit from more progress in their problem solving this term.

Your child needs to work on applying their problem solving skills across a range of different contexts.

Your child could improve their problem-solving skills by practising at home with you.

Your child sometimes has difficulty finding a solution to a problem and may need some help from an adult.

Your child could benefit from learning some more problem solving strategies. I can provide you with some recommended resources. If you have any questions or concerns, please do not hesitate to contact me.

Self Confidence

Positive

Your child is confident in their abilities and is not afraid to try new things.

Your child has a good sense of self-awareness and knows their strengths and weaknesses.

Your child is able to manage criticism well and use it to improve their performance.

Needs improvement

Your child sometimes doubts their abilities and may need some encouragement to try new things.

Your child may benefit from some extra help with self-confidence. I can provide you with some recommended resources.

Shyness

Positive

Your child is beginning to open up more and is less shy than they used to be.

Your child is starting to make friends more easily and is enjoying school.

Needs improvement

Your child is quite shy and may benefit from some extra help with social skills. I can provide you with some recommended resources.

Tardiness

Needs improvement

Your child arrives late to school more often than is acceptable. This disrupts their learning and the learning of others. Please ensure your child arrives on time for school every day.

Your child frequently has excuses for why their homework is not done or why they cannot participate in class. It is important that your child takes responsibility for their learning and completes their work on time.

Work Habits

Positive

Your child arrives to school on time and ready for the day ahead.

Your child has excellent attendance and rarely misses a day of school.

(Name) is a self-motivated student.

Your child completes all of their homework tasks on time and to a high standard.

Completes work on time and has done a great job overcoming big challenges this year.

Your child always comes to school with the necessary equipment and materials.

Has made improvements in the area of

Needs improvement

Your child is sometimes late for school and may benefit from a more regular routine at home.

Did not complete assignment on time.

Your child's attendance could be improved by ensuring they are at school every day.

Needs too slow down to improve the quality of his / her work.

Your child may benefit from some help with organizing their homework tasks. I can provide you with some recommended resources.

Grades are suffering because of missed assignments.

Your child needs to remember to bring their school materials and equipment with them every day.

Thank you for taking the time to read this report. If you have any questions or concerns, please do not hesitate to contact me.

The Above-Average Student

Your child is a top performer in our class and works hard to achieve their best.

Your child always arrives on time for school and is well prepared for the day ahead.

Your child completes all of their homework tasks on time and to a high standard.

Your child demonstrates a good understanding of the material we are covering in class.

Your child is a pleasure to have in class

Your child is always polite and respectful to others.

Your child is well behaved and follows all the school rules.

Your child is a good role model for other students in our class.

Your child is an outstanding student and a credit to our class.

The Below-Average Student

Your child is struggling to keep up with the material we are covering in class.

Your child frequently forgets to bring their school materials and equipment with them.

Your child's homework is often incomplete or of a poor standard.

Your child does not always arrive on time for school and is often disruptive in class.

Your child needs to improve their behavior and follow the school rules.

I am concerned about your child's progress in our class. Please talk to me so we can discuss how we can help your child at home and at school.

The New Student

Adjustment

Your child is new to our class this year and is settling in well.

Your child is making friends and enjoying school.

Your child is working hard to catch up with the material we are covering in class.

Your child may benefit from some extra help with homework tasks. I can provide you with some recommended resources.

Behavior

Your child is always polite and respectful to others.

Your child is well behaved and follows all the school rules.

Your child is a good role model for other students in our class.

Academic Progress

Your child is working hard to catch up with the material we are covering in class.

Your child may benefit from some extra help with homework tasks. I can provide you with some recommended resources.

Your child is making good progress in their learning.

Your child demonstrates a good understanding of the material we are covering in class.

End of Year Evaluation

Positive

Your child has made excellent progress this year and is performing at a high level. I am confident they are prepared for next year.

As we approach the end of the year, your child is well prepared for the next grade.

Your child has demonstrated a deep understanding of the material covered this year.

Your child completes all of their homework tasks on time and to a high standard. I have no concerns about their preparation for the next grade.

Needs Improvement

Your child has made satisfactory progress this year and we would like him/her to spend time focusing on his/her math over the summer break.

Your child has made satisfactory progress this year. However, we would like him/her to focus on his/her writing skills over the summer break.

Your child has made good progress this year but we would like him/her to focus on his/her reading comprehension skills over the summer break.

Your child has made little progress this year and we are concerned about his/her readiness for the next grade. I recommend that he/she attends a summer school program and receives extra help with math, reading, and writing.

End of School Messages

It has been a pleasure having your child in our class this year. They have made excellent progress and we wish them all the best for the future.

Thank you for your support throughout the year. We hope you have a lovely summer break and we look forward to seeing you next year.

Thank you for entrusting us with your child's education. We have enjoyed having them in our class and we are confident they will do great things in the future.

We wish you all the best for the summer break and we look forward to seeing you back at school in September.

Thank you for everything. Your child has made incredible progress this year and we are so proud of them. We wish them all the best for the future.

Evaluation Not Possible

Due to _____, I was unable to evaluate your child's progress in _____.

I was not able to get a good sense of your progress in your child's _____ due to _____.

In this instance I was not able to grade your child in _____.

I do not have enough information about your progress in _____ to give a report.

Please see me after class so we can discuss your child's progress in _____.

No report card comments would be given in this instance.

Useful Adverbs To Describe Student Progress

Adjectives are not the only words that can be used to describe student progress. Adverbs can also be very useful, especially when it comes to report card comments. Here are some adverbs that you might want to use:

Greatly

Vastly

Significantly

Remarkably

Noticeably

Slightly

Increasingly

Substantially

Considerably

Useful Adjectives To Describe Student Progress

Progressing well

Making good progress

Steady progress

Positive progress

Encouraging progress

Consistent progress

Pleasing progress

Satisfactory progress

Unsatisfactory progress

Inadequate progress

Progressing slowly

Lack of progress.

Conclusion

Report card phrases can be a helpful way to communicate with parents and guardians about a child's progress in school. However, it is important to use report card phrases thoughtfully, so as not to overwhelm parents and guardians with too much information or cause them undue concern. When in doubt, focus on the positive aspects of the report card, such as areas of improvement or praise.

We hope we have saved you hours by using and adapting our phrases to suit what you want to express. Please remember to leave us a review online if this book has helped you!

www.ingramcontent.com/pod-product-compliance
Lightning Source LLC
Chambersburg PA
CBHW050322010526
44107CB00055B/2355